EYEWITNESSES TO THE PASSION

Five Lenten Dramas

BY ALAN HANSON

C.S.S Publishing Co., Inc.
Lima, Ohio

Reprinted in 2003

Scripture quotations are from the New Revised Standard Version of the Bible, copyright
1989 by the Division of Christian Education of the National Council of the Churches of
Christ in the USA. Used by permission.

Library of Congress Cataloging-in-Publication Data

Hanson, Alan.
     Eyewitnesses to the passion : five Lenten dramas / by Alan Hanson.
          p.   cm.
     ISBN 1-55673-387-9
     1. Lent.   2. Holy Week.   3. Drama in Christian education.
4. Drama in public worship.   I. Title.
BV85.H34   1992
246'.7—dc20   91-26549
                                                                                  CIP

For more information about CSS Publishing Company resources, visit our website at
www.csspub.com or e-mail us at custserv@csspub.com or call (800) 241-4056.

9205 / ISBN 1-55673-387-9

To Mary, Maren,
Kirstine and Jeremy

Table Of Contents

The Most Beautiful Sacrifice

Lenten Drama One

SETTING:

Lights dim, except for center area of the stage.

A woman appears, wearing shawl or head covering, carrying an opaque flask or vase and a towel. Throughout the drama, she should be busy, or talk as she works. Perhaps other props might include table and water basin, food and utensils.

TEXT:

Mark 14:1-16

CAST:

A woman from Bethany

A man in the congregation who will sit among the people in a place where he can stand and be heard.

TIME:

Her testimony is timeless, although the events she describes occurred before Jesus' death.

WOMAN: It is almost that time of year again. The Passover, it's coming, you know. But I suppose that doesn't mean as much to you Gentiles as to us Jews, does it? Of course not. But that's not important; because I want to tell you about one special Passover I remember. One that will never be forgotten.

(Pause)

9

Oh, I must remember that I set this aside (the flask). It's important to my story. But before I tell you my story about what happened on that one Passover long ago . . . maybe you ought to understand about my faith. My papa once told me that being Jewish means that

(With emphasis)

you never forget to remember and that you never remember without sacrifice.

Remember and sacrifice. Sacrifice and remember. That's what Passover is, basically. We remember the Lord's deliverance of Israel out of the house of bondage in Egypt by sacrificing the Passover lamb. To remember God Almighty. That's the first word of the Torah.

Like Papa said, "You shall always remember God and you shall never remember without sacrifice." You know something, maybe women understand this business of sacrifice better than men; no? What do you think? That women, especially women of my station in the world, and mothers — who raise children as well as work the fields or tend the house and their menfolk — perhaps know more about sacrifice than the chief priest Caiaphas himself. It costs to remember. To remember your children, to care and nourish them, requires daily sacrifice. And should they forget or turn away from you, what a terrible sacrifice a mother pays for her love and memory.

(Pause)

I remember the day when we realized what the sores on Papa's hands were, the blisters that would not go away. Oh, it couldn't be! I remember the day when the priest said it plain — leprosy! My father! He could no longer work, or even live in Bethany. Papa was forced to live in the caves and hovels outside of town, no one allowed to touch him or kiss him.

10

We carried food out to the leper colony and left it beside the road for him, and everyone considered him afflicted and punished by God. "What sin did your papa commit to offend the Lord God so?" It was said, "Simon the leper has disgraced his family." Because my father could not work, our family nearly became beggars. We worked all day and night for money for food and wool. Talk about sacrifice! Ha! I myself had two jobs, working fields at day and in the evenings scrubbing floors in the houses of tax collectors and Roman officers. Are you shocked? But since I, the daughter of Simon the leper, was already considered "unclean" by many, being in the homes of Gentiles and sinners didn't matter to me anymore. But I made plenty of money and saved nearly two or three denarii each week. But I confess I became bitter and angry at God. "Why did you forget us, God?" I cried. "Why my father? Papa always remembered the Sabbath and the Torah. He always remembered the stories of the prophets and recalled them to his children. Why did you forget us, God, and make me a servant to pagans? How long, Lord, before you remember your promise of love?"

And then Jesus came to Bethany. You know who that is, don't you? I thought so. It was Jesus who healed Papa. Oifey, did he stir up this town! Healing and preaching, and he even raised Lazarus from the dead, right here in Bethany! Did ever any prophet cause such commotion? And the way he did it — no magic or potions or solemn ceremonies — just his word, "Be healed. Rise up! Your faith has saved you!"

Jesus healed my papa, just as Papa knew he would when he came. Papa was so grateful — so happy! In fact, he still calls himself "Simon the leper" to people.

(Chuckle)

You should see people's faces when he greets them with a hug saying "Good day, I'm Simon the leper of Bethany!"

In shock they blurt out, "But you're no leper!" "Yes, because Jesus healed me, because the Lord saved me."

Jesus changed our whole lives. With Papa able to work again, our family prospered as never before.

(Pause)

Another memory of Jesus was in the synagogue. Jesus was reading the prophet Isaiah aloud, and even from the back of the balcony, where women were allowed to sit, I could clearly hear him: "The sovereign Lord has filled me with his spirit. He has chosen me and sent me to bring good news to the poor, to heal the broken-hearted, to announce release to captives and freedom to those in prison (Isaiah 61:1)."

It was then that I realized that this man was not just any prophet or miracle worker, that Jesus was the Anointed One — the Christ of God. God had not forgotten his people. In fact, Jesus was God's way of remembering his promise. It was like living at the time of the Exodus must have been, a time of great excitement at God's power and rule ready to break upon us and rescue us. Remembering the Passover took on a whole new meaning.

But it was a frightening time, too. Because people from all over Israel, indeed all over the world, were coming to Jerusalem. Many, many thousands were crowding into the city and everywhere the talk and rumors were about Jesus. Would he be proclaimed the Jewish King? Would he oust the Romans and Herod from power? It was frightening gossip, because we all know how the authorities deal with Jewish patriots. And as many of us as believed Jesus to be God's servant, there were as many who believed he was just a troublemaker, or worse.

So as Passover grew near, Jesus promised to stay one evening with us in Bethany, just outside of Jerusalem. My father decided to throw a big party. I mean it was as royal as any feast in Judea that week. And because I knew Jesus would want to spend the Passover with his disciples in Jerusalem, I decided this was my one — maybe my last — chance to do something for Jesus.

So I gathered together the money I had saved during the years of Papa's infirmity — more than 300 silver denarii - and went to the Phoenician merchant in Jerusalem. There I purchased some fragrant nard, a very expensive spice from the distant East beyond Persia. Usually it is only kings who receive such perfume. It came in an exquisite alabaster flask sealed with wax.

(Pause, handles the flask)

Its fragrance reminded me of the Song of Solomon . . . I wanted to give to Jesus something worthy of the Messiah; something appropriate to remember all he had done for me and my family.

So then during the banquet I took the flask over to Jesus and broke it open. Jesus, like most of the guests, was reclining, so I had him sit up on his knees.

I did not begin in the customary way of my people, to wash and anoint the feet of your guest of honor with perfume or olive oil. Instead, I emptied the entire vial over his head. The nard oil ran down his hair and through his beard and onto his shoulders and robe. With the first drops, the entire room was filled with the aroma! How magnificent it was. It turned a lot of heads, I'll tell you! Jesus remained still and silent. But how people gasped and stared, and buzzed and bickered . . .

A MAN IN THE CONGREGATION *(Stands up and interrupts her description with a loud complaint):* You know very well why they were shocked, too! You are talking about

13

incredible waste here: 300 denarii . . . two years' wages . . . for what? No one, especially Jesus, needs your fancy perfume. But there are many poor people who need the money. Why didn't you remember them?

THE WOMAN *(In an angry voice):* Who are you to preach to me about the poor, or the oppressed? Do you know what it is to be poor? Do you know what it feels like to be a second class citizen? *I do!* I understand why the poor flocked to hear Jesus, while the rich trembled. I'm a daughter of Abraham and the daughter of Simon the leper living in a Roman occupied province, so before you accuse me of forgetting the poor, ask yourself what sacrifice have you made lately on behalf of the disadvantaged?

(Softer)

As Jesus said, helping the poor is always available to us, a constant vocation of the believer. But you do not always get another chance to express love to someone special.

(Pause and more reflective)

I anointed Jesus with nard as much out of fear as out of thanksgiving. Fear that I might never have another chance to show him that I loved him, that I remembered his healing of my father, and that I remembered the words of Isaiah about the coming Messiah. I was afraid evil men might try to destroy Jesus once he got into Jerusalem for the Passover. No matter what happened I wanted him to know I remembered him as my beloved King, and myself his devoted subject. And like Papa said, you do not remember without sacrifice. I was afraid, but Jesus was not. He knew what was ahead and was still confident.

When some of the other guests reproached me for my extravagant gift, Jesus defended me and said something mysterious, and frightening. He called my anointing of him a beautiful thing, but then added, "She has done what she could. She has anointed my body beforehand for burial."

This scared me, because that was not what I had intended at all, and yet Jesus considered that my royal nard, a gift for a king, was a spice for burial. But what more could I do, or say?

Jesus looked at me and said to the group, "Truly, I tell you that wherever the good news is preached in the whole world, what she has done will be told in memory of her."

(Lights fade to dark)

15

Bloody Hands, Troubled Soul

Lenten Drama Two

SETTING:

The nave should be dark, except for the dim light in the chancel area. There is an altar or table in the center of stage, on which a chalice and loaf are placed.

Judas should appear out of the darkness, using a side door close to where the people are sitting, and begin his opening remarks from there. Throughout the rest of the drama he may roam freely throughout the chancel.

Judas should be darkly, but not shabbily, dressed.

TEXT:

Mark 14:(10-11), 17-50

CAST:

Judas Iscariot, a man, probably in his 30s.

TIME:

Sometime after the betrayal. Judas is speaking posthumously.

(Judas enters in the shadows, by a side door)

JUDAS: I overheard someone here in prayer, just a moment ago. Someone here was saying, "Why me? Why is this happening to me? Why am I in so much trouble?" You don't have to deny it, or pretend otherwise . . . I know that prayer.

19

The first time I met Jesus was in Galilee, by the sea. I had come all the way down from Judea. There was a large crowd, from Galilee, Judea, east of the Jordan, even from Tyre and Sidon. All because they had heard about him. They wanted to touch him, or they wanted his hands upon their heads, or placed over their injuries. They even brought children for him to bless.

That was a huge crowd, and after a long day with them, Jesus withdrew to a hill nearby, and there he chose his disciples — "apostles" he called them. And he called me. Out of the hundreds, nay, thousands to pick from, he chose me. (I have often wondered why. What did he see in me?) And then Jesus gave us authority to preach, to cast out demons, and to anoint and heal the sick. And he sent us out — two by two — to execute this authority.

It was the most exciting time of my life. My hands, my voice . . . were the instruments of God's kingdom. Even though none of us really understood who Jesus was — Messiah, prophet, future king (?) — but there was no denying HIS authority. It was like being commissioned by Moses, or Elijah. We were the judges of old, heroes of God, saving people from their trouble and bringing them the news of God's Word.

I will never forget the way the crowds pressed in upon us and around Jesus. Once in Galilee, Jesus was asked to come to the house of a man named Jairus, whose daughter was sick. Because he was an important leader at the synagogue, the whole town was curious, and followed along hoping to see another miracle.

As we were walking, suddenly Jesus stops. "Who touched me?" he said. "What do you mean, who touched you?" we said, "The crowd is all around us, jostling and pushing to be next to you?" But Jesus would not go any farther, and insisted on finding who had touched him. And then a woman stepped forward and confessed it was she . . . She had come to be healed, for she had been suffering from an internal hemorrhage. She had been bleeding on the inside for 12 years. No physicians had been able to help her except to take her money. No one would have anything to do with her because she was ritually unclean. She did not want to disturb Jesus, or risk anymore rejection; but thought if she could just sneak through the crowd and touch the hem of Jesus' robe, perhaps that would be enough to heal her illness. And, in fact, she had felt healing inside of herself as soon as she touched Jesus. She was sure of it. Now, face to face, Jesus said to her, "Go in peace. Your faith has saved you."

How often I have thought about that woman, who was bleeding on the inside, and yet still dared to reach for and touch Jesus. On that last day how often I wished I could turn back time, and go back to the Garden — not to sneak up with a mob and a kiss, but to go alone and just touch his robe while he prayed. I bleed on the inside, too, even if I do not admit it.

Why am I, Judas Iscariot, the betrayer? Why didn't I have the faith of that person in Galilee to seek his touch and be healed? Why does that woman in Bethany have the faith to sacrifice 300 silver pieces on nard to anoint Jesus, while for a measley 30 . . . I . . . Father of Abraham, have mercy on me! Spare the knife!

It is very troubling to me. Like the person I overheard earlier whispering, "Why me?" — I don't understand my guilt; shame and trouble overwhelm me.

In the beginning it was very exciting. The crowds were large and enthusiastic, especially when we entered Jerusalem. But more and more it also became frightening. There were more expectations, more volatile situations and more opposition. Some people wanted to touch Jesus, but more and more just wanted to get their hands on him, if you know what I mean.

Even Jesus' own family thought he was crazy; others thought he was possessed; and his hometown considered him a fraud.

Jesus spoke openly about this. On three different occasions he predicted that "the Son of Man must be handed over to sinners and be rejected and killed." Another time he warned us: "You yourselves must beware. You will be arrested, beaten and made to stand before the authorities and then you will preach. Do not worry: the Holy Spirit will tell you what to say. But brothers will betray brothers, fathers will hand over their own children. But you must hold on to the end."

The religious leaders were the stiffest opposition. And Jesus was most angry at them, although at the same time he had pity on them for their hardness of heart. They, too, were afraid of the crowds. And I think Jesus was nervous enough to stay outside of Jerusalem much of the time that last week.

I will not tell you any excuses — I went to the scribes and the leaders of the temple. I told them I would let them know when Jesus was alone. They were worried about their people recognizing him, especially in the dark. I fixed that, too, providing a signal for them, . . . a kiss.

(Judas moves to the altar, or table, on which a chalice and loaf have been placed.)

That night Jesus and the 12 of us shared the Passover. While we were eating, Jesus told us, "One of you will betray me!" Everyone was afraid — am I the one? they all asked. I thought, "My God! Is everyone else like me? Are we all thinking the same thing?" Wouldn't it be ironic if all of these disciples were planning to turn him in?" It seemed to be just as he predicted would happen to us — brother betraying brother.

I had the feeling we were all caught up in something much larger than ourselves, something more important and compelling than my little schemes of self-protection.

22

"The Son of Man will die as it is written," Jesus said. "But woe to the one by whom the Son of Man is betrayed! It would have been better for him if he had not been born."

That sounds like a terrible judgment, I know. It is. But, strangely enough, at that moment I also heard it as a caring word; it was so true. Jesus understood exactly how I came to feel that night . . . wishing that I had never been born.

(Judas may lift chalice and bread from the altar.)

On the night I betrayed him, Jesus took bread, and blessed it. "Baruch Adonai Elohenu . . . This is my body." And then he took the cup, "Baruch Adonai Elohenu . . . This cup is the New Covenant in my blood. I tell you I will not drink wine again until I drink it new with you in the kingdom." Here he was, within a few hours of betrayal, arrest, torture, trial; knowing that his useless disciples would desert and scatter, still speaking about God's rule, God's new promise, still teaching about God's forgiveness and new life. Breaking bread with his so-called apostles, giving us *himself* really, putting his life into our hands: "Here, this is my body and blood." We sang a hymn and went out into the night. Jesus was distressed and anguished. He was not afraid of letting us know that. I know he would want to be alone for several hours to pray — with no crowds — and that there would only be some exhausted disciples with him. It was time . . . .

Why did I do it? I could try to give you some justification for what I did. I could say that I was disillusioned about Jesus, that I thought I was doing the right thing but was misled, that I thought that this would help our cause by bringing things to a confrontation, or that I was just plain greedy: pick any motive you want!

The fact is, there is no reasonable explanation. I don't know why I betrayed him! Why did I hand over to ruthless men the

One who had chosen me to be his apostle? Why did I turn in the most loving and righteous person I had ever met?

Ask yourselves why? What would it take for YOU to sell out Jesus? What reasons do you give yourself for your premeditated acts of betrayal, what explanations when you wake up the next morning with bloody hands, and a bleeding soul?

My biggest mistake is that I forgot where to go with this sorrow in my heart. I forgot that I was not only Judas the Betrayer, but also Judas the Chosen disciple. Do not forget that in your anguish. He chose you. Everything that happened on that terrible night happened for you! Don't forget that. Remember this: that Jesus is the soul who carries our troubles. That his are the bloody hands, which take away the sin of the world.

(Lights fade)

True And False Prophecy

Lenten Drama Three

SETTING:

The temple courtyard of the high priest.

Caiaphas, entering from the sacristy or the front, will be at a podium or pulpit in the chancel throughout the drama. Everything about his posture and voice should suggest authority edged with arrogance and pomposity. He will be dressed in elaborate vestments or robes, ideally with a Velcro fastening which will make a noticeable tearing sound at the end of the play.

Peter will enter from the rear of the nave, and will stay outside the chancel throughout the play. He will be dressed in working clothes, perhaps carrying a staff.

Although this is like a dialogue, the two men are not addressing each other, and do not even recognize the other's presence. After Peter has entered, as one talks, the other freezes.

TEXT:

Mark (26-31) 53-72

CAST:

Caiaphas, high priest, mid-50s or older.

Simon Peter, a fisherman and disciple, probably age 30-40.

TIME:

After Jesus' arrest but before his execution.

BACKGROUND:

This drama was originally titled "The Lies That Served God's Purpose." Here are two men of seemingly opposite perspectives about Jesus, but neither of them realizes the full truth of Jesus' words, and both of them will bear false witness against him in order to protect themselves or their interests. At the same time, whether out of hatred or love, both men prove to be prophetic in much of what they say about Jesus, albeit unknowingly. This is especially true in the case of Caiaphas. This drama seeks to accomplish what the Gospel of Mark portrays so well — the irony of Caiaphas' words as well as Peter's denial, as they happen simultaneously during the trial of Jesus before the Sanhedrin.

CAIAPHAS: I am Caiaphas. I speak for the people of Israel. Nothing changes for us. We have been a kingdom without a king for many generations . . . a people trampled on by the pagan nations for six centuries. Yet while Gentile empires come and go, the people of God remain, and the Word of the Lord endures forever. The whole world may change, but the Torah of God, and the tradition of our people does not change. And so, the issue for us as a people is one of keeping the faith, the preservation of our heritage in the face of a heathen and hedonistic culture which surrounds us.

As high priest, I represent what is stable and enduring. My vestments are a tradition in themselves, from the time of Aaron such vestments are worn only by the high priest on the Day of Atonement. I alone enter the Holy of Holies and offer the sacrifice prescribed by the Torah Law. This is part of keeping the faith for us; of preserving our identity as the people of God. And preserving identity is very important when you are a Jew, for we are a scattered people, and a people whose homeland is occupied.

Now I must admit, if it is God's will that we be occupied, then I am more content that it be Rome than some of the other Gentile empires which have subjugated us throughout history. Roman control has meant relative peace and stability for two generations now. Despite temporary outbursts in the population, our people's lives and livelihood and our well-being is firmly secured by the procurator. And behind him is the power of Tiberius Caesar, and behind them all, the Roman legions.

Fortunately, Rome has been tolerant of our faith and our traditions. They allow us to keep the sabbath, even when serving in the army. They exempt us from ceremonies of worship toward the emperor which are offensive to us. They even allow us to collect a temple tax, not only in Palestine but throughout the Diaspora for the support of our holy work here. We believe we deserve such special considerations and we will work hard to maintain them. Let the Romans keep the peace with justice, and we will keep the faith with proper zeal and patience. Let the Romans have control, and we will preserve our identity.

Consistency is important. We must not let the zealots, the rowdies, the troublemakers or the so-called messianists destroy what we have sought so hard and so carefully to preserve; in order that future generations may know God's unchanging Law.

PETER: Brothers and sisters! Fellow Jews! And all of you who fear God: I am Simon Bar-Jona, or "Peter" to my friends. And I am here to speak for Jesus, who I believe is the Anointed One, the Christ long awaited by our people. I am here to tell you that Jesus is a sign that everything has changed for us. Well, God has not changed, but our way of thinking about God has. It is clear to me now that it is not the kingdoms of Rome or Herod, or even the Sanhedrin which matter, but that Jesus is in control. I know this because I have seen his power exercised over demons and storms and illness, and I have heard the authority of his teaching challenging sinners and righteous alike. Let me tell you, I have had to do a lot of rethinking about who I am as a Jew and what I believe. Take the sabbath for example.

CAIAPHAS: The sabbath is an example of how important the Torah, the law, is to our identity as a people. Keeping the sabbath holy is one of the marks which separates us from the pagans. The Lord God himself set aside the sabbath for rest, for the quiet and thoughtful reflecting on his words. Only God is the Lord of the sabbath, and this Jesus of Nazareth continuously violated the sabbath codes.

PETER: One sabbath day we were walking with Jesus through a grain field, and being more than a little hungry that day, we were plucking some of the ears from the end rows set aside for sojourners, rolling and threshing it in our hands. Some Pharisees who happened to see it complained, "It is unlawful to do this on the sabbath." But Jesus asked them, "Haven't you ever read about how David entered the house of God and ate the bread of the Presence and also gave it to his men? That was not lawful either." Then Jesus told them, "The sabbath was made for people, not people for the sabbath; and the Son of Man is lord even of the sabbath." Let me tell you, the scribes and Pharisees from Jerusalem didn't like that very much!

CAIAPHAS: And another thing, Jesus and his small ragtag group of misfit followers had no respect for the authority of the Sanhedrin, the Council of Elders in Jerusalem. By law, both our tradition and Roman law, the Sanhedrin had authority over the religious matters in Judea and Samaria. And yet when directly confronted by righteous men, Jesus simply continued his practices of pronouncing forgiveness on sinners, healing and preaching and — doing so on the sabbath as well! Now tell me, is not God the only one who possesses such authority? Then, who does this Jesus think he is? And it was clear, that such a dangerous person as this must be silenced before the authority of the Sanhedrin — indeed the temple itself — be destroyed.

PETER: Once when Jesus had taken us to the villages around Caesarea Phillipi, he asked us "What do people say about me? Who do they say I am?" And so we told him. "Some say you're John the Baptist returned; others say Elijah or one of the prophets." Jesus then asked us, "But who do *you* say that I am?" And I said right out,

(Each word very deliberately)

"You are the Christ."

(Pause)

And Jesus told us not to tell anyone about this.

(Shrugs)

Instead he told us something that I could not accept. He said that the Son of Man — he himself — must suffer many things, be rejected by the elders and chief priests, and be killed, and after three days rise again. He insisted that it was necessary that he be condemned and put to death.

CAIAPHAS *(Speaks simultaneously with Peter [See following]):* We were getting more and more concerned about the crowds. In fact, many on the Council feared that a so-called miracle worker like Jesus might stir up the malcontented sections of society enough to cause a riot, or worse, a war-provoking incident. Expectations about Jesus were running high and we feared that if messianic delusions got out of control the Romans might bring calamity upon us all! So I told the scribes and Pharisees of the Council, again and again, so that there would be no misunderstanding, for the sake of our people, we must do whatever it takes. It is better for one man to die, than for the whole nation to perish.

31

PETER *(Simultaneously with Caiaphas [previous]):* We were getting more and more concerned about the crowds. Many of us among the 12 worried that the Herodians or the elders on the Sanhedrin who hated Jesus might try to stir up the crowd against us, or that zealots and malcontents might start a riot and try to make Jesus a king by force before we were ready. Expectations about Jesus as the Son of David were running wild toward the end. And it did not calm my nerves any to hear Jesus say "I did not come to be served but to serve, and to give my life as a ransom for many."

PETER *(Solo — after a pause):* He reminded us how the prophet Zechariah had said, "I will strike the shepherd and the sheep will be scattered." But when Jesus predicted that we would all desert him, I protested. Not me! Even if I'm the only one left, even if I have to die, I said, I will never deny you. And Jesus said, "This very night, before the cock crows thrice, you will deny you know me three times." No way, I told him. All of us said the same.

(This is a painful admission, filled with shame.)

But when Jesus was arrested, we all ran. When it was safe enough I followed the mob at a distance. I even dared to go into the courtyard of the high priest right outside of where Jesus was on trial. I was so afraid, I didn't see how I could be able to stand up for Jesus against the power of the elders and chief priests. But it wasn't the powerful Sanhedrin which frightened me into panic; it was a maid from the courtyard who saw me warming myself by the fire and said to me, "You were with that Nazarene, Jesus, weren't you?" I told her she was wrong, I didn't know what she was talking about. I retreated to the gateway and I heard her tell someone else that I was with Jesus. And I denied it again. Then another person said, "You're a Galilean, you must be one of his disciples." And I cursed and swore and shouted, "I do not know this man!"

(Covers his face)

O God, forgive me! Jesus was right; I don't know him!

(Leaves in despair)

CAIAPHAS *(Alone):* Finally, through the assistance of one of his pitiful disciples, we were able to arrest Jesus away from the crowds and at night and bring him before the Sanhedrin. At first our efforts to prove his blasphemy through witnesses were unsuccessful and disorganized. This gratuitous testimony was getting us nowhere. But I was confident that Jesus' own words would condemn him. However, Jesus just stood there. Silent. "Have you no answer to make?" Silence again, like a dumb sheep being shorn of its fleece, I thought. Finally, I asked him directly: "Are you the Messiah, the Son of the Blessed God?" and Jesus said "I AM." The whole company of elders gasped when he took the Lord's name on his very lips and said "I AM," and then he even dared to add "And you will see the Son of Man seated at the right side of the Almighty and coming with the clouds of heaven."

(Caiaphas tears his robe and slowly speaks.)

That's it! We don't need any more witnesses! He has said enough.

(Lights dim)

Hail!
Your King!

Lenten Drama Four

SETTING:

One platform, or chancel area, should have an ornate chair in the center for the Pilate's throne.

A bowl of water and a towel should be on a table somewhere on the stage. Near it, a sign with the words, "King Of The Jews."

At the edge of the chancel, front center stage, there will be a stand for the cross. The cross should be substantial in size but not too difficult for an actor to hold it on his shoulder and carry it. The cross may be placed in one of the aisles toward the back but not so far that people will miss any of Simon's monologue.

TEXT:

Mark 25:1-32

CAST:

Simon the Cyrene, father of Alexander and Rufus (perhaps the Rufus mentioned in Romans 16:13).

Guard, young and strong. (The same actor may portray the Centurion in Drama Five.)

Pontius Pilate, governor or Judean procurator serving under Tiberius Caesar.

TIME:

The day of the crucifixion.

BACKGROUND:

Both Pontius Pilate and Simon of Cyrene are "used" to carry out Jesus' execution. Both, to different degrees, are accomplices to his murder and both are, in a sense, bystanders, somewhat indifferent, as far as we know, to what happens. Nevertheless, their intimate and yet detached participation in the crucifixion is a powerful message in itself. But the hearer should not be able to remain a casual or indifferent observer.

Mark's account of Jesus' trial before Pilate is the most terse of the four gospels. Matthew, Luke and John each have their own unique additions to the trial story; and Luke and John are especially kind to Pilate, who in those accounts tries three times to acquit or release Jesus. But in Mark, Pilate appears shrewd, calculating, perceptive and finally, uncaring about what happens to this man Jesus. Pilate acts out of expediency, even though he is sure the accusations are false. There's a certain ruthlessness suggested as well as weakness in bowing to "popular demand."

---

*(Simon enters, looking up and around
as if excited about the big city.)*

SIMON: Jerusalem! How I love this city! Like the Scripture says: "O Zion, the mountain of God is high and beautiful; the city of the great king brings joy to all the world!"

It is indeed a sacred place and it is such an exciting time to be in Jerusalem. During Passover, the streets are crowded and festive. The beautiful buildings seem to shine because of the color and joy of the people — faithful people who have come from all over the world to be in Jerusalem for this remembrance of the Exodus.

I, myself, have come all the way from Cyrene, on the other side of Egypt in Northern Africa. It is a long journey, but worth it. I made the trip once before with my father when I was a young man, and so I promised my sons years ago that someday, somehow, we would go to Jerusalem together for Pesach — that's the name we Jews call the Passover. This will truly be a great experience for the three of us. We are staying with relatives who own a small vineyard a few miles outside the city, and have had such a good time. I expect we will stay as well for Pentecost, the harvest festival.

(Pause)

However, there have been some tense moments, too.

(Aside, hushed)

You may have heard about the riot that happened and the murder of a Roman soldier by some of the zealots. It was Barabbas, and the Roman soldiers arrested him. So the authorities are very nervous and don't want any more trouble.

And then several days ago — I did not see it myself, but I heard about it — a man from Galilee named Jesus entered the city being proclaimed King! Oh yes! Even riding on a donkey colt like the ancient kings of old, with people shouting HOSANNA! and spreading palm branches and garments on the ground! Can you believe that? That could be very serious business. I have not seen this King Jesus yet, but . . .

(Hushed again)

I hear he has hundreds of armed followeers all ready to seize power. But that is probably just talk. Who knows? Anyway, I hear that the Roman procurator has come up from Caesarea personally with reinforcements, just to make sure nothing gets out of control.

39

But I plan to stay out of their way, and mind my own business. I am not one to start trouble or get involved in politics. Live and let live is my motto. Like the Scriptures say: "The wise man is determined to live right, but the wicked man will die."

(Simon sits down in an aisle seat. Lights dim and then grow brighter again. The guard enters through main doors, goes to center area, and orders all to stand. He will repeat the order, more insistently if necessary, until the congregation does stand.)

GUARD: All stand for the Imperial Procurator! Hail Caesar!

(After everyone is standing, Pilate enters and strides quickly to the platform where his chair is situated. He may begin his monologue even before he sits. Guard motions for everyone to sit after Pilate is seated.)

PILATE: Jerusalem! How I loathe this city! Especially at this time of year. The streets are overcrowded with foreigners and natives alike, with all manner of fanatics to incite unruly mobs. I wish I could be back in Caesarea, or better yet, in Rome.

This is a frustrating assignment. Sometimes I wish Pompei had never conquered this province, in spite of the revenue it brings the Empire.

(Stands)

You see, I am a soldier, a career Roman officer trying to be an administrator to over a million people. I am not a theologian or a diplomat. I am not even particularly religious. And I am certainly not an expert in Jewish ideology. To tell you the truth, I could not care less about the theological differences between their Pharisees and Sadduccees and whatever.

40

I don't care who their prophets and messiahs and baptizers are. All I care about is that they obey the law and pay their taxes. That's it.

Every province in the Empire has its various gods and priests and philosophers, and we Romans govern them all with justice and order. The problem with this province is the fanaticism of the religion, especially their so-called prophetic hopes for a Christ — a Jewish Savior who will rescue them and be an invisible king. HA! Well, whenever these christs pop up they are clearly nothing more than lawless thieves, terrorists or violent egomaniacs. Procurators from the time of Herod have had no trouble squashing them. It is my job to put down such outbreaks as quickly as possible.

If only it were so easy, though. Dealing with the local Jewish community is a very touchy business. As I see it, the Sanhedrin, or council of elders, wants all the benefits of Roman government — the roads, the engineering, the law and order — but none of the responsibility. They complained to me that there wasn't enough water in the city. So I built a 40-mile aqueduct into Jerusalem and then they complain when I paid for part of it out of the temple treasury, despite the fact that it is by Roman dispensation that they can collect the temple tax in the first place.

I remember when I first came to Jerusalem. This is an example of how fanatical these people are about religion. Naturally when I entered the city I brought the Roman standards with me, carrying the imperial eagle which is the symbol of our emperor. I even rode in at night so as not to cause undue attention or hostility. But still the Jews protested that I had brought Roman idols inside their holy city. They said it was an abomination and violated their commandment against graven images.

(Shrugs)

41

Day after day crowds were demonstrating and raging on, until finally I ordered my troops to draw swords to scare them off. But, get this, they literally bared their necks like this,

(Demonstrates)

perfectly willing to be slaughtered like chickens rather than have Roman standards inside their gates. Since then I've learned religion is a very serious matter with these people. Same thing with this incident with Barabbas and Jesus.

Recently there was a riot in which one of my troops, among others, was killed. We rounded up a number of typical zealot revolutionary-types, Barabbas among them, who I intended to execute in a very public way to cool any future lawless tendency in the crowds.

Then first thing this morning, Friday, here comes the Sanhedrin with this Nazarene named Jesus. They have him all bound up in chains and they're in a big hurry to have me try his case. The chief accusation is that Jesus proclaims to be the Messiah, the King of the Jews, and they say he is a dangerous enemy to the province. So I ask this Jesus, who by the way looks no more dangerous than my wife, "Are you the King of the Jews?"

And he says, "You say so." Now what kind of an answer is that? But that's the only thing he said, in the face of all kinds of accusations and throughout my interrogation, he would not deny or affirm. He kept silent. Amazing!

But I could tell that the Sanhedrin was eager to (how do you say it now?) railroad this man into prison or whatever, because they were jealous for some reason. And as is customary at Passover I could present the people with the option, Barabbas or Jesus, and if the people, the crowds, chose to release Jesus, then I'd be off the hook with the Sanhedrin.

But the crowd wanted what the Sanhedrin wanted. They all demanded that Barabbas be released. Then what do you want me to do with this "King of the Jews?" I could whip him, or run him out of town, lock him up? What do you want? "CRUCIFY HIM!" they shout. For what? At least with other messiahs there's been a proven crime — murder or arson or theft or at the least vandalism. With this man there's no evidence of crime. He hasn't even spit on the street! But the crowd kept hollering "CRUCIFY HIM! CRUCIFY HIM!" What am I supposed to do?

(Washes his hands in the bowl)

I don't like to see murderers go free, but it was a case where it was out of my control. I had to release Barabbas and put Jesus in his place, or else there might have been another riot and a lot of people hurt or killed. Just one of those instances of fanatic religion. And sometimes, even Roman justice has to take a back seat, for the good of the many.

(Dries his hands)
(Pilate continues, mocking, flippant)

After all, how many procurators have the responsibility to execute the "King of the Jews?"

(Takes the sign and hands it to the guard)

Centurion, you have your orders!

(Pilate starts to leave)

GUARD: Yes sir. Sir, the man is already beaten pretty badly . . . What if he cannot carry it the whole way?

PILATE: You have your orders . . . .

(Pilate is gone)

43

(Guard looks down the aisle. He grabs Simon from his chair to carry the cross up front.)

GUARD: You, come with me!

SIMON: No, please, I have my sons. I don't even know this man. I haven't done anything.

GUARD: If he can't carry it, you will. Take it up and fall in.

The cross-carrying will be very slow and deliberate. Simon will speak but the guard will remain unaffected, as these are Simon's inner reflections. He pauses after each thought.)

SIMON: Good Lord, so this is Jesus! I never would have thought . . .

(Shudders)

He bleeds all over. Oh, why am I here? I never had anything to do with him. Why aren't his disciples here? Why am I the one following him up this God-forsaken hill? This is not how I expected to spend the Passover!

Please . . . the people are spitting! Stop it! I'm not the guilty one.

(Pause)

Now they make fun of me, too! I didn't do anything! I hate this, Ugh, this beam is heavy. It grows heavier by the second. But even heavier is the loneliness. It's so disgraceful and . . . lonely to be here . . . so humiliating, and dark. Probably the only one who knows what I feel like is this Jesus. But he doesn't say anything. He walks and bleeds. And I follow and carry this awful thing. I doubt that I, or my boys either, will ever be able to forget this. What a King he has turned out to be! He wears a crown of thorns. His throne is this cross. How incredible that some people thought this man was the King of the Jews. Last Sunday the crowd shouted his praises. "Thou art Holy, enthroned on the praises of Israel." But no one sings his praises now . . . only jeers and insults.

(Arriving at front center stage, he plants the cross.)

Oh, why am I here? I guess someone had to help him, poor man.

(Then, as a second thought)

Help who? Help the Romans crucify him? Oh Lord, I really did not want to become so involved.

*(The guard and Simon watch the cross for
a few moments as the lights slowly fade.)*

My God, My God, . . . Why?

Lenten Drama Five

SETTING:

There is a cross in the front center stage.

Only the backlights are on.

See diagram on page 50 which shows actors' paths across the stage.

The centurion is standing holding a spear.

Mary Magdalene is the least obvious and is standing or leaning against a far wall.

Joseph of Arimathea is seated under the back lights which have cast the cross and the two other witnesses in silhouette.

Each character speaks in turn, but oblivious to the others.

TEXT:

Mark 15:33-47

CAST:

Centurion, a strong-looking man whose bearing suggests leadership and confidence.

Mary Magdalene, dressed darkly. She has been a close follower of Jesus.

Joseph of Arimathea is a wealthy, dignified, learned and pious individual. He is a wise elder who can look at an event from different perspectives. Mark describes him as "a man looking for the kingdom of God." For purposes of contrast (and inclusivity), he is portrayed as elderly.

TIME:

The day of the crucifixion.

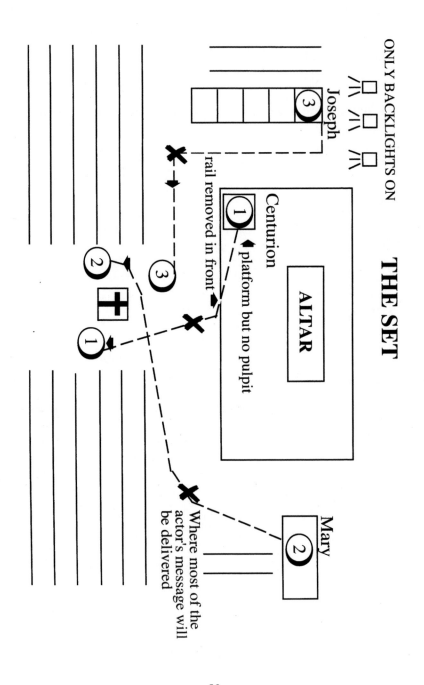

THE SET

ONLY BACKLIGHTS ON

Joseph

Centurion

ALTAR

platform but no pulpit

rail removed in front

Where most of the
actor's message will
be delivered

Mary

50

(When the lights come on, the centurion will be in obvious silhouette on the raised platform. He will speak plainly in a matter-of-fact, confident tone, but his words will carry conviction and a sense of awe.)

CENTURION: I have seen a lot of crucifixions in my career, many carried out under my command. I did not expect this execution to be any different, but it was. At the time, when this Jesus of Nazareth was handed over to our battalion, morale among the troops was dirt low, because of the riot, you know. And even worse, because that murderer Barabbas had been let go! There were a lot of hot tempers over that.

So when this Galilean was brought in on charges of being "King of the Jews," the men sort of took out their frustrations on him. They dressed him up like a pretend Jewish king, robe, scepter, crown and all . . . and then proceeded to beat the . . .

(Stops himself)

I'll admit I joined in on the 'entertainment.' Look, I just follow orders. And it's not unusual to rough prisoners up a little or make sport of them. Sometimes they deserve it, believe me. With Jesus, however, it was more than that . . . like revenge, if you know my meaning.

(Clenches fist, intensely)

This so-called "King of Judea" made a perfect target for us to get even with Palestine.

(Then lightens up)
(Moves to middle stage)

But what was amazing was not just that this man survived the beating, and all the humiliation that went with it, but it was how he suffered.

51

Not once did I hear from his mouth the quaint Hebrew names and curses that I've grown so accustomed to hearing in Jerusalem. He never tried to strike back, even in words. But while his mouth was silent, his eyes spoke often, but not with hatred. He seemed to look right through me, through my cruelty and my pretending to be tough, and looked at me. His eyes showed pity, not for himself, but for all of the characters around him who were caught up in this crazy thing.

(Pause — moves a little closer)

Do you know how a person dies on a cross? Sometimes, often, it takes two or three days. Some say it's the exposure to the sun that kills them. Some say it's the loss of blood, or maybe the person's own suffocating weight constructs and exhausts the lungs. Some say it's really the slow torturous bites of a thousand insects, which cannot be swatted away. You know, all that . . . but it's the loneliness and humiliation that kills them off, it breaks down their spirit. Minds deteriorate in time. Victims lose control. Almost always.

Not Jesus, though. He lasted only six hours of crucifixion. The beatings had weakened him. But I remember thinking: What courage this man has! He is not a religious nut; he's more like a brave soldier following strict orders, and he's determined to carry them out to the letter. He refused to drink any of the drugged wine we give to the condemned to dull their senses. He continued to remain silent despite all the pain and insults directed at him by the mob. And I thought to myself: Whose orders is he following? Who is it that could give such orders, a command to face such a death, and have them obeyed so completely?

(Moves next to cross)

And suddenly, about 1500 hours, he cried out! I was surprised he had so much of a voice left. It was no whimper either.

52

More like a battle cry or salute. Even though I don't know Hebrew, somehow I understand what he was saying, something like

(Loudly)

"Hail God! Hail God!"

Then he died.

It was in that silence that I heard what this Jesus was saying. It was in the darkness that I finally saw who he was. This was no ordinary man, pretending to be an ordinary king. This was a man who was truly the Son of God!

(The centurion freezes beside the cross. Gradually Mary Magdalene comes out of the shadows, her head covered with a shawl. She speaks with lots of emotion; meekly at first, but then assertively.)

MARY MAGDALENE: This is a nightmare. Why is it so dark in the middle of the afternoon? It is like all creation has become a tomb . . . .

(Shudder)

I have never seen a person crucified before. I always stayed away from such things because I believed it was unclean, that even to see it was a defilement. Oh, but now, how I would run to him if the guards would let me, and kiss his feet and hold him!

(She moves to center mark, behind cross but still visible to audience.)

For many months several other women and I have followed him, and assisted Jesus and the 12 in their ministry. Jesus was

53

hope to us. Hope for a new Israel, a new life, a new world. His words meant healing and faith, acceptance and forgiveness. For myself, Jesus' presence meant freedom.

My life was no longer captive to fear and anxiety.

Now this . . . horror. Along with the one who loved us most dies our hopes. With Jesus, our faith is nailed to a cross. The God of our faith . . . dies, and leaves us alone in the dark.

Like Jeremiah the prophet said, "Have you completely rejected Judah? Does your heart loathe Zion? Why have you struck us down so that there is no healing for us? We look for peace, but find no good; for a time of healing, but there is terror instead."

We, the daughters of Jerusalem, have become like numberless widows whose bridegroom has been murdered on his wedding day.

We, the people of Israel, are like the sky whose sun has gone down at midday in shame.

(She moves closer to the cross, opposite the centurion.)

Just before he died, Jesus cried out, "Eloi, eloi, lema sabachthani!" Some thought he was calling for Elijah. So did I at first, and hoped that what some rabbis had said about Elijah would come true, that the prophet would return to rescue a righteous man in distress.

But then I realized that Jesus was quoting the psalm, "My God, My God, why have you forsaken me?" Why indeed?

That's what I want to know! Why? Why is the one who was caring and truthful hanging on the cross, while evil men ridicule him?

54

Why is Jesus on the cross and not Barabbas? Why not Pilate? Why not Caiaphas or Herod? Why not Judas or Peter?

Oh, Jesus, why is it that I have this haunting feeling that you hang there in my place? Oh, my God, that is truly the deepest and darkest pain of all.

(She stands motionless opposite the centurion.)

(Joseph of Arimathea has been seated, reading the Scriptures silently to himself. After Mary is finished, he stands to speak and moves slowly toward the people and the cross. His face, too, will be obscured by the shadows. But he will be carrying the Scriptures open in one hand and a lamp or candle to read by in the other.)

JOSEPH OF ARIMATHEA: I have been looking for a long time. Like the rest of my people, I am waiting for the Messiah, hoping and praying for God's kingdom to come.

Today I have also been looking for answers — perspectives and understanding on what happened to Jesus outside of Jerusalem on Golgotha. And I came upon this reading in the prophet Amos: .

(Reads Amos 8:9-10)

"On that day, says the Lord God, I will make the sun go down at noon, and darken the earth in broad daylight. I will turn your feasts into mourning, and all your songs into lamentation; I will bring sackcloth on all loins, and baldness on every head; I will make it like the mourning for an only son, and the end of it like a bitter day."

Such judgment is not what I was hoping for. You know I really cannot count myself as one of his disciples. But I sincerely wish it could have been different for Jesus and different for the people of Israel.

55

(Shakes his head)

A very sad day.

(Stares at his book, then into the distance.)

You have probably heard that I was the one who buried Jesus. It's true. Somebody had to!

(Shrugs)

His disciples have all disappeared, except for a handful of women. His enemies on the Sanhedrin were hoping the buzzards would take him. And the Romans, . . . well, forget it!

(Shrugs again)

So I went to Pilate the procurator, and reminded him that it was contrary to Jewish law that a dead body be left hanging overnight, especially on the Sabbath. Once he was sure Jesus was dead, he released the body into my care. Pilate knows who I am, and he did not care whether I was related to Jesus or not. And if some of my colleagues on the Sanhedrin want to complain about Jesus being buried in so fine a grave, eh, let them.

At least Jesus received a decent burial. Because the Sabbath was coming we did not have time to prepare and anoint the body as fully as we would have wished. But two of his followers, women who had watched him die, helped me wrap the body and place it in the vault.

As I folded the linen around him, . . . Ach, he was so young and strong, I recalled how vigorously he used to preach about the kingdom. His stories and parables were so fresh and powerful.

"The kingdom of heaven is like a mustard seed, the smallest of all seeds, which grows into a great bush and a home for all the birds of the sky."

And, "the kingdom of heaven is like the tiniest bit of yeast hidden in a batch of dough, being kneaded and worked, while it invisibly spreads to leaven the whole loaf of bread."

(Pause)

Jesus also posed a new and special challenge to me. Once he said to us, "It is easier for a camel to go through the eye of a needle, than for a rich person to enter the kingdom of heaven." "Who then can be saved?" a disciple asked him. Jesus replied "For flesh, it is impossible; but all things are possible with God!"

(Smiles at the memory and sighs)

All things are possible!

But if all things are possible, Jesus, then why did you come to such an ignominious end? Why did not God send his hosts with Elijah or Moses at their lead to deliver you?

(Joseph turns toward the cross)

Please believe me, Rabbi. I mean no disrespect. But does it not seem ironic, even tragic, that the one who had many of us believing that the age of miracles had returned, did not save himself? And where is the Spirit of prophecy now? The kingdom seems invisible again.

(Joseph turns toward the cross)

On the other hand, if Jesus is the true messenger of the kingdom of God, or more, its Messiah, then this cross spells the end of many of our ways of thinking about life and death, about law and justice, even of our ideas about religion, charity, piety and mercy. All that we assume is right and good has been called into question. But God has chosen to act mysteriously before, right?

(Mildly amused)

After all, he called Abraham, didn't he? And Jacob and Moses?

Perhaps I've been looking too long. And maybe I shouldn't be surprised if the glory and honor and power of the kingdom of God is found, or finds us, in the person of a simple carpenter's son:

A master, who chooses to serve . . .

A healer, who chooses to suffer . . .

(Ponders it)

Hmmm, a suffering servant.

(His face suddenly lights up as he understands. Then begins thumbing through his Bible to Isaiah 53 and reads it aloud, verses 4 and 5.)

Let me see . . . Yes, here it is: "Surely he has borne our infirmities and carried our diseases; yet we accounted him stricken, struck down by God, and afflicted. But he was wounded for our transgressions, crushed for our iniquities; upon him was the punishment that made us whole, and by his bruises we are healed."

This is the Word of our Lord.

(Joseph blows out his candle, and the lights go out.)